Bertha Spafford Vester

FLOWERS OF THE HOLY LAND

BERTHA SPAFFORD VESTER

Flowers of the Holy Land

30 Color Reproductions
of Original Watercolors

With a Biographical Sketch
by Lowell Thomas and a
Note by Norman Vincent Peale

HALLMARK CARDS, INC., KANSAS CITY, MISSOURI, 1966

© 1962 by Hallmark Cards, Inc.
Library of Congress Catalog Card number 62-14859

PRINTED IN THE UNITED STATES OF AMERICA

FIRST PRINTING, SEPTEMBER, 1962
SECOND PRINTING, MARCH, 1963
THIRD PRINTING, SEPTEMBER, 1964
FOURTH PRINTING, JUNE, 1966

Distributed to the book trade by
DOUBLEDAY & COMPANY, INC.
Garden City, New York

CONTENTS

5

A Lover of Nature; a Botanist; an Artist with True eye for line and colour; Mrs. Vester has given us a very beautiful work.

I have had, more than once, the good fortune to see the miracle of Spring in Palestine; and these illustrations recall, vividly, the splendour of that season.

In accuracy of detail, in brilliancy of colour, and in correct grouping, Mrs. Vester has achieved a triumph; and her art makes it easy to understand how even the glory of King Solomon was outdone by these lilies of the field.

Anyone who has visited Palestine in the season of flowers will want the book,

Lord Allenby (1861-1936) was the British commander who liberated Jerusalem from Turkish rule on December 9, 1917. For an outstanding military career, he was promoted to field marshal and raised to the English peerage.

as a reminder of the vision.

Those who have not yet seen that gorgeous display will be irresistibly lured to the hills and valleys where such wonders exist; and this book will enable them easily to identify each bloom, from the sinister-looking black arum of Samaria to the honeysuckle familiar to us in English hedgerows.

Allenby F. M.

Cairo.
_16. IV. 25._

While in Jerusalem, Lord Allenby saw and admired Mrs. Vester's watercolors of Palestine's wildflowers. He suggested the paintings be put in a book and asked if he could write an introduction. This is Allenby's original manuscript. A printed version is on the following page.

7

A lover of Nature; a Botanist; an Artist, with the eye for line and colour, Mrs. Vester has given us a very beautiful work.

I have had, more than once, the good fortune to see the Miracle of Spring in Palestine; and these illustrations recall, vividly, the splendour of that season.

In accuracy of detail, in brilliancy of colour, and in correct grouping, Mrs. Vester has achieved a triumph; and her art makes it easy to understand how even the glory of King Solomon was outdone by these lilies of the field.

Everyone who has visited Palestine in the season of flowers will want the book, as a reminder of the vision.

Those who have not yet seen that gorgeous display will be irresistibly lured to the hills and valleys where such wonders exist; and this book will enable them easily to identify each bloom, from the sinister-looking black arum of Samaria to the honeysuckle familiar to us in English hedgerows.

Allenby F. M.

Cairo,
16.IV.25

8

Photograph Courtesy of G. C. Henderson

BERTHA SPAFFORD VESTER

My Most Unforgettable Character

by LOWELL THOMAS

It was three years ago, in September 1959, that the television program "This Is Your Life" went to work on me. The cameras caught me by surprise at a public dinner and, as some viewers may remember, I wasn't too happy about it. But the whole thing was suddenly made right when in walked Bertha Vester—who had come all the way to New York from Jerusalem. I threw my arms around her and told the master of ceremonies and all those watching millions, "Now *this* is somebody whose life you ought to tell about!"

In my time I have met many remarkable personalities, but Bertha Vester is one of the few I have ever envied. Now 84 and as active as ever, she is an American who has lived a dramatic life in that most dramatic of cities—Jerusalem—helping others. She has known kings, princes, field marshals—and thousands of humble people, Muslims, Jews and Christians, who call her, simply, *Ummuna.* In Arabic that means "mother of us all."

What has Bertha Vester done? What *hasn't* she done! As a child, she was formally adopted by an Arab tribe. Once she mercifully amputated a Turkish soldier's arms (although she hadn't the slightest medical training). It was she who furnished the white surrender flag used when Jerusalem fell to the British in 1917—part of a hospital sheet! She stoutly faced death in heavy gunfire during the fierce battles of 1948. A gifted painter of Palestine's wildflowers, she has also written a book called *Our Jerusalem.* She speaks a bewildering number of languages, including perfect Arabic. Above all, she has devoted her life to Jerusalem's babies and children—teaching them, caring for them. She runs a famous baby hospital, probably the finest of its kind in the Arab Middle East.

I first met Bertha Vester in 1918, shortly after Field Marshal Allenby and his British troops captured Jerusalem from the Turks. She was 40 then, a lovely woman with stunning auburn hair. I was struck at once by her grace and poise, her wit and quick mind. Already a long-time resident of Jerusalem, she knew everything and everybody there, and the British conquerors flocked to her for advice. I heard at least one British officer refer to her, in fond jest, as "the Queen of Jerusalem."

She had been brought to the Holy City at the age of three. Her father, Horatio Spafford, a prosperous Chicago lawyer, and her mother, Anna, were deeply religious people who underwent a series of family tragedies. After four daughters were drowned and their only son died of scarlet fever, the Spaffords decided to put the vanity of the world aside and, with Bertha and her baby sister Grace, live in Jerusalem, giving service to others. A few Chicago friends joined them, so that there were 16 in the group that Horatio Spafford led into dusty, Turkish-ruled Jerusalem in September 1881.

Jerusalemites soon began calling the newcomers the American Colony, a name which still persists. The Colony's hero was the Good Samaritan, its by-laws the Golden Rule. The women nursed the sick, taught Arab and Jewish mothers how to take better care of their children. "What they did was settlement work, although the word hadn't been coined yet," explains Bertha Vester. "Father held Bible study classes, but he taught English, too, and nursing. And he also introduced the eucalyptus tree into this almost deforested land."

The Spaffords won the confidence of the Arabs as few foreigners have ever done. As I walked into the American Colony Hotel one day, a black-shrouded Arab woman passed me—"My sister," Mrs. Vester said. She told me how one day shortly after the Spafford family arrived in Jerusalem, they innocently picnicked on private land. The young Arab owner came up and was dumfounded to find Mrs. Spafford feeding baby Grace from a bottle. His own mother had just had twin baby girls whom she couldn't nurse, so that they were about to die. Mrs. Spafford showed the mother how to use condensed milk in a nursing bottle. The twins lived and became lifelong friends of the Spaffords: the "sister" I had just seen was one of them. And, a wonderful touch of continuity, this "sister's" *granddaughter* was operated on just recently in Bertha's splendid baby hospital.

Bertha was a very small girl when her father took his family into Bedouin country to visit Sheikh Ali Diab Adwan, ruler of the important Adwan tribe. The half-wild tribesmen had never seen a white child. They were enchanted with Bertha, wondered at her russet hair, ate salt and bread with her (a pledge of lifelong friendship) and formally adopted her into the tribe as "Murtha," the closest they could come to her first name. This too has been an enduring tie. In 1950 the great-grandchild of Sheikh Ali Diab was a patient in her hospital. And still, every now and then, an old sheikh will come up to her in the street, peer at her with dimmed eyes and ask, "Is this not Murtha Adwan?"

As a young woman Bertha helped run the city's only school for Muslim girls, until 1904, when she married Frederick Vester, son of a German Lutheran missionary. The couple devoted themselves to the work of the American Colony, enlarged by then with nearly 100 new members and under the direction of Bertha's widowed mother. Frederick put the Colony on a sound business basis—with gift shop, hotel, a pig-raising venture, even a car agency—the profits meaning more money for good works.

Then World War I burst on Jerusalem. The U. S. consul urged the Colony members to leave, but Bertha's indomitable mother said firmly, "We came to serve, and this is our supreme moment for service." As her health began to fail, more and more of the Colony's work fell to Bertha, who was now 36 and had six children of her own.

Because of wartime shortages and Turkish disorganization, Jerusalem was full of near-starving people. With funds from American friends, Bertha set up soup kitchens that eventually were feeding 2400 people daily. After the United States entered the war, the Germans forced their closing, claiming they were "American propaganda." But the Turks, through the Grand Mufti of Jerusalem, asked Bertha to run *their* soup kitchens

"They were a scene from the Inferno," she told me. "Hundreds of ragged skeletons, fighting each other to get a scrap of food! Only policemen with whips kept the people from tearing each other apart."

Yet Bertha Vester walked into that starving, fighting mob and clapped for silence. She reminded them how the Colony's kitchens had been run and promised to do the same here if they would cooperate—with enough food for even those at the very end of the line. Eventually she was feeding 6000 people every day, without police or whips.

After a bitter and bloody battle at Gaza, thousands of wounded men, British prisoners as well as Turkish soldiers, were brought into Jerusalem. "I saw them lying unattended on stretchers in the road," Bertha Vester once said to me. "I couldn't stand it." With her husband, she called on the dreaded, unpredictable Djemal Pasha, who held life-and-death powers over Jerusalem. He was curt and ungracious; that very day the United States had severed diplomatic relations with Turkey.

"And you," he thundered, "are still willing to nurse our wounded?" Bertha Vester answered, "We plan to nurse neither friend nor foe—only humanity." Touched, Djemal Pasha turned over a Turkish hospital to the couple. They took on another, and another, until they were running four. Now Mrs. Vester added surgery to her skills. Once she amputated both arms of a Turkish soldier who had had a grenade go off in his hands; another time she removed the eye of a soldier wounded by a bullet. "I had to," she says. "There was nobody else."

The fighting ended on December 9, 1917. "About seven in the morning our doorbell rang," she told me, "and there stood Hassain Effendi al Husseini, mayor of Jerusalem. He said, 'I am on my way to deliver the letter surrendering Jerusalem to the English, and I want your mother to be the first to know.' We all sang the Doxology—the Muslim mayor, too—thanking God for the end of the war. Mother warned the mayor not to go without a white flag of truce, so I picked up a hospital bed sheet, tore it in two, and attached it to a stick." This was the historic flag which surrendered Jerusalem to the first Christian army since the Crusades.

A chance encounter led Bertha Vester to start what may be the most important of all her good works. On Christmas Eve, 1925, she was leaving for Bethlehem to lead the first carol singing ever held in the fields where "shepherds watched their flocks by night" when a young Arab woman, supported by her husband, approached. The man had brought his ill wife six hours on donkey-back to the general hospital—to find it closed to out-patients because it was the Christians' Christmas holiday! Inside a bundle of rags the woman was carrying a baby only a few days old.

"Frankly, I was anxious to leave for the caroling. Then the thought struck me: here right before me was a rustic madonna, very ill, and metaphorically, with no place for her or her child at the inn, either."

Bertha Vester got the sick mother admitted to the hospital immediately. But at her gate next morning she found the Arab husband waiting, with the baby. His wife had died in the night. He held out the infant, saying, "If I take him to my cave, which is my only home, he will surely die."

She had no facilities for caring for babies but, hesitating only a moment, Mrs. Vester said, "I'll take him."

17

Within a week she had two more babies handed her. So she hired a nurse, arranged for a Jewish woman doctor to check them, and thus began Bertha Vester's famous baby hospital.

Today this hospital—named the Spafford Memorial Hospital in honor of her parents—includes a complete surgical department and an outpatient Infant Welfare Center. It is housed in what was the original seat of the American Colony. Her strong right arm is a Muslim Arab physician, Dr. Mahmoud Dajani, recently joined by his young cousin, Dr. Hassan Dajani, who earned his certificate in pediatrics from the University of Pennsylvania Graduate School of Medicine. Dr. Mahmoud Dajani and Mrs. Vester share a firm belief in the power of prayer. Just before an operation, Dr. Dajani may telephone her: "Can you come help me pray? This is going to be a tough one." They pray together, in their different ways. "Asking the same God," she says, "for strength and wisdom."

Mrs. Vester still goes to the baby hospital regularly. She points with compassion to an infant so wizened by starvation as to seem more like a baby monkey. "If only," she says, "we could get young American interns to work here, for six months, even three! They'd see diseases they now know only from books, like this infant pellagra."

18

Next is a little girl suffering from a serious form of chorea (St. Vitus's dance). "Her parents took her to a sorcerer," Mrs. Vester explains. "Only when she was near death did they bring her here. She'll leave in a few days, completely cured."

During the savage Arab-Jewish fighting of 1948, Mrs. Vester took her babies to safety outside Jerusalem. The American Colony's buildings were hit repeatedly and many of the helpers wounded. Since the Armistice this section of the city, the Old City, has been part of the Arab nation of Jordan, separated by a no man's land from the rest of the city in the new nation of Israel. Early in the fighting, Bertha Vester had set up an impromptu casualty clearing station in the Colony's main building. After the Armistice Arabs who had formed the habit of going there for treatment kept on coming. So Mrs. Vester established an outpatient clinic for adults. A few years ago during anti-American troubles, one tourist, seeing what looked like a mob gathering, asked, "Is this another demonstration?" It was simply the normal assemblage of sick Arabs waiting to see the doctors. The clinic is still going strong, with demands on it increasing daily.

In the old sense of a religious group, the American Colony of Jerusalem no longer exists. After Anna Spafford's death in 1923, members split away. Perhaps the time for such colonies had passed. All the Colony property, since it was held in common, was divided among the members by a British court. Bertha and her sister were awarded the building which is now the baby hospital, and the larger Colony center, which Mrs. Vester today runs as the American Colony Hotel. Its profits support the surviving colonists, now of great age, and pay some of the costs of Mrs. Vester's charities.

At 84, Bertha Vester's brain is still churning with plans for the future. American Colony Charities Association, the U. S. fund-raising committee for her projects, has unfortunately never been able to provide enough additional money for all her philanthropic needs: hospital, infant welfare center and adult outpatient clinic. The clinic, for example, does what it can, but of the 60,000 patients last year, about one-third required hospital care.

"We need a general hospital here so desperately," she sighs. "What a wonderful thing if it could be an American one!" A committee already owns a 15-acre site and a U. S. architect has offered to draw up plans. Because of Jordan's low building costs, a 100-bed general hospital could be built and equipped for perhaps a fifth of what it would cost in the United States.

Though that hospital is yet to be built, a brand-new masonry work has just been completed in Jerusalem's Old City where hardly a stone is moved without official sanction. It begins at Herod's gate and wanders up and around the heights, along ancient "streets of steps." What's new is that each step has been filled in

20

for part of its width with concrete, making one side of the stairs a ramp. Mrs. Vester, no longer young, could not be expected to climb daily all the steep wearying steps to her hospital, and there was no way to drive there. Now she can be pushed in her wheelchair up what is known as "the incline of the great Sitt (lady)." It is, perhaps, the most touching of all tributes to Bertha Vester.

Mother of Mercy

by NORMAN VINCENT PEALE

One encounters some truly memorable people in this life, rare and unique individuals who make an indelible impression. Such a personality is Bertha Spafford Vester. Without doubt she is one of the most remarkable human beings I have known.

Mrs. Vester is a curiously fascinating combination of gentle femininity and rugged force. In appearance she is fairly tall with stately carriage; she has fair skin, blue eyes and snow-white hair. She is without at all intending it a commanding person, not in manner or speech, but in an indefinable impact of personality. Yet there is a kindly gentility about her, a radiance, that not only endears her to people but inspires them as well.

Though her life has been set in an area and in a time of almost continuous conflict—Jerusalem during World and regional wars—she has had the balance and fortitude to live creatively and at the same time with peace in her mind and love in her heart. She is one of those persons who has handled rather than been handled by the vicissitudes of life.

This of course has been made possible not only by a rugged indomitability but also and primarily by a deep religious faith. She was reared in a Christianity-in-depth home atmosphere and this experience really took. It built up in her a doubt-free faith that has demonstrated vitality and sustaining quality when the going gets hard, as indeed it often has in her eventful life.

This same faith also activated in Mrs. Vester a profound love for the unloved and a deep compassion for suffering humanity. Little wonder that the Arabs today call her "Mother of Mercy." Every morning she may be seen among the poor and the sick who crowd her clinic to the astonishing number of 70,000 persons every year. Anyone who needs help gets the immediate assistance of Mrs. Vester.

A heavily-veiled Bedouin woman once approached Mrs. Vester—she was hiding something which proved to be a terrible tubercular sore from her ear to her breast.

"It will cost much money for the medicine alone —$500 to cure this woman—and we just haven't got it," said the doctor to Mrs. Vester.

"Yes, I know," was Mrs. Vester's answer, "but the woman must be healed. So start the treatment. I will pray, and as He has done before, God will send the money."

24

"Did He?" I asked.

Her merry eyes twinkled. "Don't you believe there are still Good Samaritans? I prayed, and a few days later there came a letter from America. And what do you think it contained? A check for $500! Some would say that's coincidence, but since such 'coincidences' have been happening in our work for 75 years, I came to the conclusion it's the law of prayer and human need."

But it is in her Spafford Memorial Baby Hospital that the character and love of this woman are best observed. On successive trips to Jerusalem I have visited all the sacred places of the Holy Land. In common with all pilgrims I have been stirred by the privilege of walking where Jesus walked. But none of these experiences moved me as deeply as to walk with Mrs. Vester and her faithful Dr. Mahmoud Dajani from bed to bed in the children's hospital. They knew every child, calling each one by name. How the eyes of those youngsters lighted up as she touched their heads or patted their cheeks. Most of the diseases of childhood are represented there, but malnutrition and undernourishment are at the bottom of most.

"How do you do it?" I asked Mrs. Vester. "How do you restore so many to healthy life with such limited facilities?"

She answered simply, "He once walked these very streets among sick little ones like these. And He said,

'Suffer little children to come unto me and forbid them not'."

Her hospital for babies and little children is Christianity in current action. I felt the presence of an alive Christ as we passed from bed to bed looking into appealing little faces.

Mrs. Vester, who carries on in modern days the Master's work of healing and helpfulness, has stimulated a love and compassion that brings Jesus Christ closer to the heart than any ancient landmark can. Through her gracious ministry of compassion the Great Physician is evidenced.

There was one unforgettable moment when I truly felt the Presence. It was one day when we drove with Mrs. Vester to Emmaus, that little town where Jesus, after His crucifixion, appeared to two disciples as they walked. Now this village is on the tensely guarded border between Jordan and Israel. We humbly hoped that we too might "meet" the Lord on the road to Emmaus. As we neared the border, Jordanian soldiers stopped us politely but a bit sternly. Then the husky sergeant saw Mrs. Vester. He ran to her and kissed her hand. There was love and veneration in his whole attitude.

As we passed on, she explained simply. "As a child he was brought to our hospital sick unto death. We were able to save him. He is one of my babies." As she spoke, I had my meeting with Jesus on the Emmaus road. I felt His presence. Love made Him real.

I hope that someday you may visit the Holy Land. Until such time these pages will give you a taste of its charm and beauty. If you have walked its ancient pathways this volume will bring back some of the fascination you felt while there. And this book will make you acquainted with a gracious and lovely lady who in our time of pain and trouble has brought the healing touch of our Lord to so many of His little ones.

Yellow Bethlehem Star

This early winter flower grows in damp stony ground and is common especially on hillsides having a northern exposure. Although both are members of the lily family, the Bethlehem star should not be confused with the Star-of-Bethlehem which has white petals faintly marked with green on the back.

Pink Onion

First discovered near Jerusalem in 1916, the pink onion is one of about twenty-five species of wild onions in Palestine. As with the cultivated onion, the bulb may be separated into many divisions. This stout-stemmed, strongly-scented plant grows in rocky places to a height of three or four feet and flowers about May 20.

Syrian Speedwell

Common throughout the Holy Land, the Syrian speedwell blossoms in profusion in early February. Just three or four inches high, it forms a striking blanket of color on an otherwise sparse winter landscape. Its petals are either white or blue and beautifully tinted and striped.

Mountain Lily

This widespread, although not abundant, flower blooms in April. Found chiefly in clay ground, the mountain lily can be distinguished from other members of the leafless amaryllis and lily families by its foot-high leafy stem.

Jerusalem Salvia

A member of the mint family, the Jerusalem salvia blooms at the beginning of April in Syria and Palestine. It possesses the family's characteristic square stem and aromatic foliage. The plant, one of twenty members of the genus salvia found in the Holy Land, grows to a height of two to three feet.

B.S.Vester

Palestine Cornflower

The Palestine cornflower is similar to the English and American cornflower, or bachelor's button. The Latin name means "starthistle," of which Palestine has more than twenty species. Thistles and thorns are mentioned in Genesis as part of God's punishment of Adam. They grow in such enormous numbers as to take possession of whole fields in the Holy Land.

Scarlet Anemone

The scarlet anemone is one of Palestine's most striking flowers. Many people think it is the "lily of the field" spoken of in the Book of Matthew. The anemone grows in such abundance in the Holy Land that the ground is almost hidden by a mass of scarlet.

B.S.Vester

Jerusalem Crowfoot

The Jerusalem crowfoot looks like the buttercups of England and America. The plant has tiny, glossy petals of bright yellow and finely divided, greyish-green foliage. Because the crowfoot is indigenous to rocky soil, it grows in profusion in Palestine.

Polyanthus Narcissus

One of Palestine's most charming flowers, the polyanthus narcissus is thought by many people to be the "Rose of Sharon." It grows in abundance on the Plains of Sharon, Carmel and Jericho. The people value the narcissus for its very sweet odor, and bouquets of narcissus are sold in the marketplaces of large towns.

Pomegranate

Pomegranates, olives, grapes and figs have been cultivated in Palestine since Biblical times. A passage in the Book of Deuteronomy speaks of "a land of wheat, and barley, and vines, and fig trees, and pomegranates." The pomegranate grows on a small tree with bright green leaves. The fruit looks like a large apple and is filled with many seeds and a red, juicy pulp.

Blue Lupine

This flower attracts immediate attention because of its intense blue color and its hand-shaped leaves, a rarity in plants. The blue lupine fills whole fields in Galilee between Nazareth and Tiberias, creating a striking effect. It blooms in the late spring.

Almond

The Hebrew word for almond means "waker" or "watcher." The name is significant because the almond is the first tree to blossom in winter. A grove of trees in full flower is one of the Holy Land's most beautiful sights. Next to the olive and fig the almond is the most commonly cultivated fruit tree in Palestine, and almonds are exported to the corners of the world.

Pink Cistus

This large, pink flower blooms during Palestine's lovely spring. A fragrant gum, called ladanum, comes from the cistus. The gum is referred to in Genesis as myrrh—"Take of the best fruits of the land in your vessels, and carry down the man a present, a little balm, and a little honey, spices, and myrrh, nuts, and almonds."

Field Morning Glory

This particular species of morning glory is recognized by the shape of the stigma. The flowers stem from a long, trailing vine. Growing wild throughout the Holy Land, the morning glory blossoms in May and is frequently seen in fields of grain.

Pentagonia

The pentagonia is similar to the true Venus' look-
ing-glass, with larger blossoms. When grain attains its
full height in April, the blue flowers of this plant can
be seen in almost every field of the Holy Land. The
flowers are so abundant they impart a distinct blue to
the ground as one passes by.

Garland Chrysanthemum

There are four kinds of chrysanthemum in Palestine. All are yellow and look very much alike. Unlike the autumn-blooming flower that Americans cultivate, the garland chrysanthemum blossoms in March. It grows to a height of two feet or more and may be seen in fields and lowlands throughout the Holy Land.

Early Tulip

The tulip, along with the Star-of-Bethlehem, squill, grape-hyacinth and hyacinth, belongs to the lily family. There are four very large red flowers in Palestine, all resembling each other: the tulip, anemone, ranunculus and poppy. They give the land a startling beauty — magnificent color against an ancient background.

White and Purple Anemone

Anemone blossoms display almost all colors from white to purple, but the flowers are varieties of one species—anemone coronaria. These varying shades of color dot the Plain of Sharon, a fertile stretch of land ten miles from Jerusalem which has fed men and animals for countless ages.

White Mustard

This variety of the mustard family derives its name from light-colored seeds. The white mustard is a tall, stout annual with small flowers. It blooms in April in the rocky soil of the Holy Land. The yellow blossom is the most common of the several varieties of mustard. There are also white and lilac blossoms.

The pink flax is one of the three or four most abundant flowers in Palestine. Found in every part of the country, it always attracts attention because of the bright pink tinge it gives to the fields. It blossoms in the spring, during late March and early April, and gives the land a singular beauty.

Charming Vetchling

There are twelve species of vetchling in Palestine. The charming vetchling, as its Latin name "amoenus" implies, is the most delightful. A slender, climbing herb, the vetchling grows in the Holy Land's grain fields and often attaches itself to the grain stalks. The flower is large, with a yellow keel and reddish wings.

Thicket Rose

Wild roses are comparatively rare in Palestine, but are widely distributed. They climb over walls and rocks in the hill country, preferring a northern exposure and blooming in April. Another tall, climbing species with pure white flowers grows in Galilee.

Two varieties of scabious are seen in the Holy Land: one with cream-colored flowers, the other with light blue flowers. The plant is a common, stout perennial found growing on the hills to a height of two or three feet. Because it blooms so late in May, it is often taken as a sign that spring is at an end.

Corn Flag

Growing almost exclusively in the grainfields of
the Holy Land, the corn flag is indigenous to Palestine.
It blooms in early April, before the grain ripens. The
flowers, a rosy color at first, darken with age to a deep
purple. Dr. Post of the University of Beirut supposed
this plant to be the Biblical "Lily of the Field." It is
strikingly beautiful.

Daisy

The Palestine daisy grows from six to twelve inches high. Its petals are white, often tinged with pink or purple. The flower appears in abundance in damp areas of the hill country. It blooms early, sometimes at the end of October, and reaches its height early in March. It continues to flourish until the heat of summer. The goldenrod and aster of England and America belong to the same family as the Palestine daisy but do not grow in the Holy Land.

b.s.Vester

This beautiful plant, called Humhum in Arabic, grows everywhere in the rocky areas of Palestine, Syria, and Lebanon. Its botanical name is Anchusa Strigosa— Boraginaceae. The plant's tall stalks are covered with flowers ranging from white to blue. People who live in this part of the world often use Humhum leaves in poultices on themselves and their animals. The leaves are also good to eat.

Egyptian Pink

Almost three dozen varieties of the pink family
flourish in Palestine. The Egyptian pink, the most
common, often blankets with color uncultivated fields
in the Galilee Valley and on the Plains of Philistia.
The plant grows about six inches high and is one of
the first spring flowers to bloom, usually early in February. The same flower occasionally is called catchfly
or campion.

Anatolian Orchid

There are about twelve species of orchids in Palestine. The Anatolian, which blooms early in March, is found everywhere in the hills of the Holy Land. The flower takes its name from Anatolia, the Greek word for Asia Minor. The earth-wasp orchid and monkey orchid also grow in profusion throughout the Holy Land, especially in the rocky soil of the hills.

82

B.S.Vester

Storax

The storax tree is common on the hills on both sides of the Jordan, but especially in Galilee. It grows from twelve to twenty feet high and blooms about mid-April. It has large white flowers. The fruit of the tree is white-wooly, round and nutlike. The fragrant balsam obtained from the bark is used in medicine.

Prickly Smilax

The flowers of the prickly smilax are small and insignificant, but the berries that ripen in December are a brilliant shade of scarlet and remain on the sprays long after they are gathered. These berries are used to make beautiful winter decorations in the same way bittersweet and holly are used in America. First blossoms of the prickly smilax appear in the Holy Land in October and November.